NORTHERN ESSEX

Edited by Donna Samworth

First published in Great Britain in 2003 by
YOUNG WRITERS
Remus House,
Coltsfoot Drive,
Peterborough, PE2 9JX
Telephone (01733) 890066

HB ISBN 1 84460 134 X
SB ISBN 1 84460 135 8

FOREWORD

Young Writers was established in 1991 as a foundation for promoting the reading and writing of poetry amongst children and young adults. Today it continues this quest and proceeds to nurture and guide the writing talents of today's youth.

From this year's competition Young Writers is proud to present a showcase of the best poetic talent from across the UK. Each hand-picked poem has been carefully chosen from over 66,000 'Hullabaloo!' entries to be published in this, our eleventh primary school series.

This year in particular we have been wholeheartedly impressed with the quality of entries received. The thought, effort, imagination and hard work put into each poem impressed us all and once again the task of editing was a difficult but enjoyable experience.

We hope you are as pleased as we are with the final selection and that you and your family will continue to be entertained with *Hullabaloo! Northern Essex* for many years to come.

CONTENTS

Chani Antrobus	69
Colby Will	70
Ross Falco	71
Adam Gardiner	72
Lily Turner	74
Eddie Parsons	75
Claire Hills	76
Matthew Wright	77
Sam Mahoney	78
Mike Ellmers	79
Kerry Bray	80
Stefanie Klarner	81
Clare Gravatt	82
Gemma Day	83
Mitchell Freeman	84
Danny Christie	85
Amy Wright	86
Ryan Day	87
Gaby Baldock	88
Ellen Gage	89
Tom Childerley	90
Gemma Gardiner	91
Stevie Adams	92
Laura Vile	93
Annabel Shaw	94
Daniel Curme	95
Shaun Buer	96
Gabriel Saldin	97
Faye Davis	98
Laura Gilbert	99
Kirstie Grace Tominey	100
Faye Walton	101
Ami-Jane Foweraker	102

Mersea Island School

Hetty Ann Baalham	103
May Leverington	104
Daisy Sherwood	105

St Peter's CE Primary School, Coggeshall

The Poems

THE WIND

Just seeing him go past
The wind flowing through my hair,
Trees flowing and flowers blowing.

The mice hide in their holes,
You could see the eyes watching,
I got scared but would not dare to cry.

The sun hid behind the clouds,
Then the weather changed to coldness,
At last he went before my eyes.

Tori Kingsbury (9)
All Saints CE Primary School

My Dog Holly

My dog Holly sleeps on her back,
She sits really funny because her leg goes slack,
Her eyes droop when she's sad,
When she looks up to you,
Her eyes are glad.

Rowena Milwain (9)
All Saints CE Primary School

MY CAT, BERTIE

Bertie is a lovely cat,
As nice as nice can be,
She likes my strokes and pats, she does
And that's just fine with me.

Bertie is a silly cat,
As mad as mad can be
She likes to run around the house
Chasing our dog, Brie.

Bertie is a lazy cat,
As lazy as can be,
She goes to sleep in the afternoon,
But not before her tea.

Ben Grew (9)
All Saints CE Primary School

SLIPPERY SNAKE

Slippery snake slithering up a tree,
Slimy snake please do not eat me,
Slippery snake look at your venomous fangs,
Slimy snake don't dig them into me.

Crunching snake swallowing your prey,
Digested the next day,
Snip, snap every day,
Slither snake and he's away.

Samuel Mulford (9)
All Saints CE Primary School

MY DOG, BEN

My dog, Ben eats all the night,
Until the morning comes
And when the sun goes out of sight
He'll eat up all the crumbs.

My dog Ben sleeps all the time,
It seems he sleeps all day,
I think I might find it fine,
If he would come and play.

Tom White (8)
All Saints CE Primary School

MY DOG, TEASLE

Our dog, Teasle is a menace
And very naughty too,
She likes to play with her ball
And chew, chew, chew.

Our dog, Teasle is a bit sensible,
She eats all kinds of food,
Meat, fruit and vegetables,
When she's in the mood.

Our dog, Teasle is by the fire,
Sound asleep don't shove or push,
Otherwise she'll wake up,
So please *shhh!*

Dominic Daniels (8)
All Saints CE Primary School

BROTHERS

My brother can be a pain,
My brother plays with cars,
My brother gives me a strain,
But I still love my brother.

My brother dances in the rain,
My brother's really messy,
My brother plays with his train,
But I still love my brother.

My brother plays with Action Man,
My brother is really naughty,
My brother plays with his teddy lamb,
But I still love my brother.

Chloe Chapman (9)
All Saints CE Primary School

THE STRANGE CAT

There was a strange cat,
Who's friends with a rat,
He sleeps anywhere,
His head is as big as a ball,
But he is always eating meat,
He is really small,
The only problem is he is always standing on his feet.

There was a strange cat,
Who sleeps on a mat,
He always goes outside,
He loves eating fish,
There he is waiting for it on his dish.

Georgie Baker (9)
All Saints CE Primary School

MY AUNTIE'S CAT CALLED CRAVITS

Cravits is a funny cat,
As anyone can see,
She sits on your lap
And she's as funny
As she wants to be.

Cravits is a smart cat,
Smarter than any cat will ever be,
She sits on the wall
And she smiles at me.

Cravits is a loving cat,
A loving cat she is,
She makes me love her more,
By purring at the door.

Chelsea Banks (9)
All Saints CE Primary School

BUMBLEBEES

Bumblebees are yellow,
Bumblebees are black,
Bumblebees smell flowers,
With a sting on their back.

Summer's sun is shining,
The bees are coming back,
The pollen is now spreading,
The bees are getting fat.

We're playing in the garden,
I saw a bee go by,
Buzzing all around me,
In the summer sky.

Savannah Rate (8)
All Saints CE Primary School

BEES

Bumblebee, bumblebee,
Always making honey,
In a tree,
Oh it's definitely a bumblebee.

Honey bee, honey bee,
Always sitting in a tree,
In a hive making honey for you and me,
Oh what a lovely bee.

Busy bee, busy bee,
Always sitting in a tree,
In a hive making honey
Oh it's a busy bee.

Victoria Patrick (9)
All Saints CE Primary School

CATS

Cats are wonderful, they are soft and fluffy,
Charlie, Snudge, Ginger and Smoky,
They are all different,
Some are fat,
Some are skinny,
Some are just right
And I like them how they are.

Georgina Lungley (9)
All Saints CE Primary School

AUSTRALIA

Aussie was a dream, a dream it was
But now it is no more,
We're on the plane, a very long ride,
I covered my ears and tried to hide.
My ears went pop so I sucked my sweets
And then I decided to suck my feet.
'Disgusting!' said Mum, 'Err!' said Dad.
'That's not healthy that's just bad.'
What was I meant to do,
Play with my toys?
Oh I'm so bored, what do you expect,
Four planes to catch altogether,
Come on planes, we're going to be late.

Samantha Lloyd (10)
All Saints CE Primary School

WEIRD WEEK AT SCHOOL!

Monday my teacher skated to school,
Tuesday the head made no sense at all,
Wednesday the teachers jumped off the wall,
Thursday the deputy looked really cool,
Friday the sec dressed like a fool,
It's the weekend now and we all play ball,
Oh no, it's Monday again!

Bethany Mallon (10)
All Saints CE Primary School

My Garden

Come in my garden
I have posies and sweet flowers,
You can pick for hours and hours.
Come in my garden
I have a gingerbread hut,
With a roof made from sweet nut.
Come in my garden
Open the side gate,
Come in, have dinner,
Don't be late!
Come in my garden
Follow the trail,
Don't go north or you will fail.
Come in my garden
You won't go home for I have got you,
You will never roam.

Carrie-Anne Chapman (10)
All Saints CE Primary School

PEOPLE

Girls
Girls are spoilt
Girls are brats
Girls are very scared of rats.

Boys
Boys are handsome
Boys are cool
When girls look we stare and drool.

Adults
Adults are bossy
Adults are stroppy
All they say is don't be so sloppy.

Jake Race & Connor Read (10)
All Saints CE Primary School

BUBBLEGUM

You see it under tables,
You see it under chairs,
You even see it on
Big escalator stairs!

You get it on your elbows,
You get it on your knees,
Everyone gets it on them . . .

. . . but the mighty fleas!

Heather-Louise Cameron (10)
All Saints CE Primary School

Boys

They're dirty things they are,
They wipe their bums with Dad's old shirts,
They hit their heads until it hurts,
They're dirty things they are.

They're noisy things they are,
They run about and scream and shout,
They're noisy things they are.

Emily Louise Sadler (10)
All Saints CE Primary School

Loo

I need the loo
And it's 10 to 2
I have nothing to do
But I need the loo.
I want to play with the hay,
I need the loo,
Mum said, 'Go out to play,
It's a sunny day,'
But I need the loo
And it's 5 to 2
And I did not want to play.

Tom Chitty (10)
All Saints CE Primary School

LITTLE FLY

Little fly upon the wall,
Have you go no sense at all?
Can't you see it's made of plaster,
Now you're stuck what a disaster!

You only came to have a look,
At all the good things we might cook,
But now you've come and lost it all,
Poor little fly stuck on our wall.

Little fly upon the wall,
Do you feel sick, please don't fall,
From down here, you look really small,
Little fly upon the wall.

Hannah Weeley (10)
All Saints CE Primary School

MY MUM WON'T LET ME KEEP A PET RAT!

My mum won't let me keep a pet rat,
She won't even let me keep a bat,
She won't let me keep an iguana,
Not even a pet piranha.

She won't let me keep a seal
And a fish that's its meal,
She won't let me keep a llama
Not even a lazy koala.

Aidan Harry Blackburn (9)
All Saints CE Primary School

DRAGON

I'm a fire-breathing monster,
I fly up very high,
I'm very, very scary
I like to dive through the sky.

Danger, danger,
My house is in flames,
I really don't like him,
He's calling me names.

The people from the village,
They always run from me,
Just like I want them to,
Running like they're free.

We people from the village,
We always run from fear,
Before we get hit
For the dragon is near.

Zoe Tibbs (10)
All Saints CE Primary School

PIZZA
(Read Fast!)

Pizza round, pizza soft,
Pizza on my plate.

Tower of pizza, pizza place,
Pizza is ace!

Ravioli is helleoli
On my plate
Always sloppy, always sticky,
Ravioli is stinky.

Spaghetti is messy,
On my plate,
Always slippery,
That's why I hate,
Spaghetti.

Gregory Land (10)
All Saints CE Primary School

HAIR

Hair is so messy,
You can curl it,
You can twirl it,
You could put it in a bunch,
Hair is so awkward, it gets tangled in your lunch,
You can cut it,
You can shave it,
You can gel it in a quiff,
Hair is hell when it goes stiff.

Jack Burkett (10)
All Saints CE Primary School

THE KANGAROO

She goes to the riverside to get a drink of water,
With a joey in her pouch,
She stands on a crocodile, she goes, *ouch*
And she goes *ouch* again.

She still goes on with a bite in her thigh,
Her baby joey goes down to lie,
She goes over the highlands on the wavy grass,
Her joey comes out of her pouch and goes very fast.

The joey is grown-up and she is a mother now,
She gets all the food for her baby,
She comes across a cow
They go hopping off in the distance.

Jack Abbott (9)
All Saints CE Primary School

My Sister

My sister drives me mad,
My sister is very bad,
My sister drives me up the wall,
My sister is so small.

My sister can be a pain,
My sister hates trains,
My sister annoys me,
My sister is as noisy as can be.

Hannah Callow (9)
All Saints CE Primary School

WORM

I can't sit still,
It's just too hard,
I squibble, squabble in the yard.

I can't sit still,
It just isn't fair,
My friend said and I declare.

I declare worms sit still,
Here take a chill pill.

They try to tell me not to squirm
But I can't help it I'm a worm!

Paige Jolly (10)
All Saints CE Primary School

MY BROTHER HENRY

My brother *Henry*
is a noisy as can be
whinging and whining
he knows it annoys me.

My brother *Henry*
he's as funny as can be
jumping off sofas
bringing the fun back to me.

My brother *Henry*
he's as naughty as can be
jumping on the dining table
he thinks he's as funny as me.

Billie Race (8)
All Saints CE Primary School

THE END

Millie was my best friend,
But it came to an end.
She had been my mate for years,
But it all ended in tears.
All because of a sweet,
That we both wanted to eat.
She said it was hers,
But I said it was mine!
She said she did not like me anymore,
So I said fine!
I feel lonely today,
I'm not so mad as yesterday.
Millie said she was sad too,
And 'I would like to be friends with you.'
And so it ends
With us being best friends
Till next time,
I suppose!

Jay Smith (11)
Boxted CE Primary School

SURVIVING SCHOOL

If you can do your work without whispering
To the person next to you . . .
If you can listen to your teacher all day and learn
Something new . . .
If you cannot daydream all day . . .
If you can listen to what your teacher has to say . . .
If you can make a better excuse than your dog ate
Your homework . . .
If the teacher tells you off and you don't smirk . . .
If you don't moan at the teacher if it's play time and
It starts to rain . . .
Then you will survive school!

Katie Weekes (9)
Boxted CE Primary School

MY TABLE

Jay sits on my table, she is very helpful,
She tells me funny phrases
And makes me laugh all day.

Millie's on my table too,
She laughs and giggles,
Like good friends do.

James sits next to me,
He's friend number three
And sometimes tells jokes
About Mrs Lait's cup of tea.

And then it's me,
I laugh with Jay
And giggle with Millie
And joke with James
And that is what we do.

Penny Smith (11)
Boxted CE Primary School

WINTER

It's a snowy time of year,
When children will appear,
Throwing snowballs at each other
And their sister and brother.

Birds are flying to the south
While you are catching snowballs
In your mouth.

Animals are hibernating in burrows and holes,
Like rabbits, hares, foxes and moles.
The summer sun is no longer near,
Winter is the best time of year.

Maddie Weekes (9)
Boxted CE Primary School

THE MONSTER

The monster wails through the deserted streets,
Blowing coldly on anyone it meets,
The monster hurls litter at dirty walls,
Bawling loudly through empty malls.

The monster sends a chill down people's spines,
Pausing to sneeze at different times,
The monster now stands in the street alone,
While everyone else is safe at home.

Tom Horspool (11)
Boxted CE Primary School

MY DAD

My dad spends time reading books,
He always lights the fire,
My dad slouches about
Then goes to sell skips for hire.
My dad makes me laugh
But then turns daft,
He thinks he's a hunk
And calls me 'Chunk.'
My dad wears jogging bottoms,
Except when we go out,
Then he wears his smartest shirt
And puts on his deodorant,
That makes the house stink!

Dannielle Pugh (11)
Boxted CE Primary School

ALUN ARMSTRONG

It's Alun, not Alan,
The classic footballer.
He's friendly, he's funny, he's an all round man.
He's very stylish in his Jaguar,
He's great, he's magic, a family man.
He's skilful, an Ipswich fan,
He's a golden shot, a passing man.
He's friends with Town, he's friends with me,
He's lightning fast,
It's Alun, not Alan,
The classic footballer.

Stephen Young (11)
Boxted CE Primary School

WINTER POEM

Because of the weather
The animals huddle together,
To keep warm,
From the winter snowstorm.
Birds fly by,
Leaves shrivel and die,
The world is white,
The children have a snowball fight,
The snow falls hard,
The whole place looks just like
A pretty Christmas card.

Millie Smith (10)
Boxted CE Primary School

ME AND MADDIE

When me and Maddie were four
I knocked on Class One's door
And that was when we met.
When me and Maddie were five
We used to jump and swim and dive.
When me and Maddie were six
We used to make houses out of sticks.
When me and Maddie were seven
She left me alone and went to Devon.
When me and Maddie were eight
We met a girl who we both hate.
When me and Maddie were nine
We went to a party that was fine.
That's our life, it's great now, then
I can't wait till we're both ten!

Rosie Aston-Prigmore (9)
Boxted CE Primary School

PARADISE

Sand slipping through my toes,
As the water from the waterfall
Aggressively flows.

Monkeys swing from tree to tree,
Knocking down coconuts
For you and me.

Sea swirling all through the day,
Washing up sparkling shells,
On the bay.

The sun glowing in the sky
As singing seagulls
Fly by.

Alexander MacPhail (9)
Boxted CE Primary School

WATER

Water comes from everywhere,
Up here and down there.
In lakes and ponds,
In taps and baths.
Up there in the clouds,
Rain isn't that loud.
Drip drop, drip drop,
Quieter, quieter, quieter,
Then it stops,
No more drip drops.

Kim Munson (11)
Boxted CE Primary School

THE LEAVES ON TREES

The leaves on trees
Rustle with the wind.
They twizzle around
Then fall to the ground.
The trees that have leaves
Sometimes have bees.
I like to walk
But not talk
So I can listen to the leaves
Falling from the trees.

Christopher King (10)
Boxted CE Primary School

SUN

The burning sun is golden
And floats around the sky.
It's there till night,
A beautiful sight.
When the sun goes down
The sky is full of beautiful, bright colours,
Pink, orange and golden yellow.
Then the world turns dark
And the moon rises into the sky,
Then everyone is sleeping soundly,
Shhh, be quiet.

Kelly Hearn (10)
Boxted CE Primary School

Boooo!

I walked along in the dark,
Holding a candle with a tiny spark.
I walk and trip over the stones, big and lumpy
Inside the castle walls.

I stop and listen to the great loud howls,
Is it a ghost?
No, I say to myself,
I try to imagine it's just an owl,
Howling in the night,
Trying to give me a fright.

James King (10)
Boxted CE Primary School

THE WORLD AROUND US

The world around is a home to some beautiful places
And in that world there are many faces.
There are the animals, colourful and bright,
There are the trees and wonderful little plants,
There are many mysterious planets in space,
Which no one knows about,
There are lakes and rivers with tiny fish,
There is a big golden ball of lava in the sky
And that is the world around us.

Shay Howe (11)
Boxted CE Primary School

THE STALLION

The black stallion all dark and mighty,
Shines in the sun like the dark sky.
Gallops over the fields and mountains
Like a black jaguar.
When he stands on the hilltops,
He rears and whinnies,
But at night he returns to the mountain's shadows
And stands like the leader,
Waiting till the sun rises again.

Yasmin Kluss (11)
Boxted CE Primary School

SCARED IN THE DARKNESS

In the darkness of the forest,
Creatures walking into bushes,
Very gloomy, very spooky,
Shadows moving I am frightened,
Trees are scary, look like people,
Loads of goblins come and chuckle,
Weary voices come from the sky,
Talking animals come near by me.

Antonya Fay (8)
Chase Lane Primary School

FOGGY WEATHER

Foggy weather
I can't see
Oh, I dread it
Falling over
Grazed knees
The things I hate
People screaming
Hooray! It is
Time to go in.

Katie Suley (9)
Chase Lane Primary School

IN THE DARKNESS

In the darkness of the forest,
Leaves are crunching, wolves are howling,
Stars are twinkling, trees are swaying,
Hands are frozen, moon is shining,
Eyes are sleepy, twigs are snapping,
Spooky shadows, creepy-crawlies,
On the treetops of the forest,
Birds perch shivering in the branches.

Lauren Rigg (9)
Chase Lane Primary School

IN OUR ANIMAL PARK

Roll up to Animal Park
Where . . .
Dolphins leap,
Kangaroos jump,
Koalas climb
And larks lark.

Why not stay all day,
Where . . .
Platypuses swim,
Snakes slither,
Gallahs fly
And dingoes play.

So why don't you play
Where . . .
Elephants eat,
Frogs croak,
Goats sleep
And horses neigh.

Don't forget what you came for
See where . . .
Yaks yackety-yak
And zebras just snore
Zzzzzzzzzz

Gabriella Barr (8)
Chase Lane Primary School

PEACE

Peace's face is a picturesque landscape of
young children running through the sweeping grass,
Her eyes are the blue of the warm summer sky,
Her hair is the long winding rivers populated
by the fast moving salmon.
Her teeth are the colour of the freshly fallen winter snow,
Her cheeks are as soft as the finest goose feathers,
but as rosy as freshly picked cherries,
She lives in the highest clouds of Heaven where the
angels sing sweet lullabies to send her to sleep.
Her enemies are war, pain and destruction
which she will conquer one day.

Laura Kington (11)
Chase Lane Primary School

PEACE

Her hair is the vines swishing side to side,
She wears the poppy petals that flower every year,
Her face is smooth angel's skin,
She eats the souls of bad people,
Her dreams are silent with no pain or blood,
She wishes that war didn't exist,
Her teeth are the pearly gates of Heaven,
She lives in everybody's hearts,
Her enemy is war.

Ashley Wood (10)
Chase Lane Primary School

ANIMAL PARK

Roll up to our animal park,
Where . . .
Toads croak,
Birds squawk,
Koalas cling
And pigs lark.

Why not stay all day
Where . . .
Elephants clean,
Foals lay,
Calves eat
And lambs play.

You'll come back for more
Where . . .
Insects crawl,
Jackals sleep,
Kangaroos lay down
And lions roar.

Don't forget what you came for
See where . . .
Yaks yackerty-yak
And zebras just snore
Zzzzzzzzz.

Eve Homan (8)
Chase Lane Primary School

OCEAN

Her hair is the beautiful coral swaying
From side to side,
Her eyes are the islands, all lonesome and small,
Her nose is the great white shark smelling its prey,
Her cloak is the water, crystal-blue,
Her food is the seaweed, enough for life,
Her husband is land, sharing the world,
Her children are the fish swimming around her,
Her enemy is oil, soon to pollute her life.

Samantha Teatheredge (11)
Chase Lane Primary School

HEROES

Bending, buckling like a sheaf of limp corn in a strong wind,
Bare, bleeding, battered feet leaving prints in the soft, squelching,
Muddy earth,
Suffering with each step the weak struggle to survive,
Weeping tears like crystals, gleaming in the candlelight,
The putrid strench of sweat and blood permeates the misty evening air,
Shrieks of pain echo as victims of death are randomly taken,
The voices of angels beckoning the heroes,
Dreaming of loved ones . . .

Emily Allen (11)
Holland Park Primary School

HARVEST TIME

A small child with a swollen belly
Crying because he's hungry,
His mother has no food or milk
To feed him, to feed herself.
There are no crops to harvest,
The cattle lie dead in the burning sun.

I don't like peas, I don't like cabbage,
I don't like Brussels sprouts!
Then leave it, says the mother,
But you won't get any pudding,
The child pushes his plate away,
Crying because he's angry,
The food is scraped into the bin.

A child cries alone in her room,
She hasn't eaten for days,
There are no cuddles, no kisses,
Father lies asleep,
Whisky bottle by his side,
All the money spent on drink and cigarettes,
The girl is forgotten,
Cigarette burns, bruised arms and legs,
One little girl's life.

I don't love you anymore,
Shouts the boy wanting sweets,
His mother says, 'No, not now.'
He's angry, she's angry,
The child stamps his feet,
Mother makes him lunch,
Mother reads him a story,
'Love you,' he says,
She cuddles him, she kisses him,
Somewhere in the distance,
A hungry child weeps.

Bridey Coffey (11)
Holland Park Primary School

THE TRAPPER

I sit alone by that massive, creaky, old door, I'm scared,
I'm scared of the ghosts that wander through the tunnels,
I'm scared of the noisy darkness,
I'm scared of the huge, furry spiders that run across my dirty hands,
I'm scared of the shadows crawling around on the walls,
I'm scared of screams from children who are injured,
I'm scared of the people creeping up behind me,
I'm scared of falling asleep because my master beats me,
I'm scared of the gas because the mine might explode,
I'm scared of dying as I sit alone by that massive, creaky, old door.

Jasmine Long (10)
Holland Park Primary School

MY APPLE'S SECRET

My rosy apple looks like the rising sun,
It is as red as my blood pumping around my body,
My apple feels as smooth as a baby's skin
And as hard as laminated wood.

As I bite into my juicy apple, it smells
Delicious like my mum's perfume,
It is as crispy as the leaves in autumn,
My sweet apple tastes mouth-watering,
Scrumptious and delightful.

Laura Oldland (11)
Holland Park Primary School

THE COAL MINE

Deep down,
Low in the dark, scary mine,
I hear the chipping of a pickaxe
As the coal tumbles slowly.
I hear the screeching of the coal trucks wheels,
I hear the crying of the trappers as they sit and
Pray to get out of here,
I hear the screaming of the patter as they pull
The big heavy carts,
I hear the rumbling of the cave's walls as
The roof caves in,
I hear the crashing of the coal,
As the walls fall in,
Deep, down, low
In the dark scary mine,
I pray I will get out of here someday.

Ryan Weeks (10)
Holland Park Primary School

REBECCA'S POEM

I miss you like a book misses its pages,
I miss you like a CD misses its sound,
Without you I'm like a witch with no cauldron,
I miss you like a fish tank misses its fish,
I miss you like a lion misses its roar,
Without you I'm like a cow with no moo.
I miss you like a door misses its handle,
I miss you like a flower misses its stem,
Without you I'm like a teacher with no pupils.
I miss you like paper misses its lines,
I miss you like a clock misses its hands,
Without you I'm like a pencil with no lead.

Rebecca Blaser (10)
Holland Park Primary School

THE TRAPPER

He sits all day
Opening and closing his wooden door,
Listening to the screaming children
Caught in the coal truck,
Hearing the cries of pain
As another child is beaten again.
As he opens and closes his wooden door
He hopes,
He wishes he could go home.
He wishes he could go to sleep in his warm bed,
As he opens and closes his wooden door,
He hopes the mine will not cave in,
He hopes there will be no explosions,
He prays to God.

Rosie White (11)
Holland Park Primary School

THE TRAPPER

He sits freezing,
Day and night,
In the dusty, dismal, darkness,
Tired and bored,
Opening and shutting his door,
Till his eyes close and his arms ache.
Trucks rumbling from end to end,
Dragged by tiny children,
Every day he hears,
Children screaming for help,
The squeaking rats scamper round his feet,
As the dynamite explodes,
As he sits freezing,
His stomach rumbles,
He thinks of all the unlucky people,
Those who died,
He wonders if the roof will cave in,
He wonders if the gas will explode,
He wonders if he will get out alive today,
He prays he will escape one day.

Darren Griffiths (11)
Holland Park Primary School

THE OAKS COLLIERY EXPLOSION

Everybody screaming, 'Get out!'
Stamping feet
People getting wedged indoors
Screaming and shouting,
Sighing
The tweet, tweet of the canary,
Crying,
Rumbling,
Crack,
Bang,
Boom,
Run, run, run,
Sweat dripping from our heads,
The crack of light,
Shining through the door,
Too late!
Bang!
We're all dead.

Matthew Dearman (10)
Holland Park Primary School

MATTHEW'S POEM

I miss you like a tap misses its water,
I miss you like a petrol can with no petrol,
I miss you like a car without wheels
And a snail with no shell.
I am like an apple without pips,
Like the sea without salt,
I am like a footballer without a football
And a toilet with no flush,
I am like a photo album with no photos,
I am like a match with no flame,
Without you I am like a clock without hands.

Matthew Fisk (10)
Holland Park Primary School

DANIEL'S POEM

Without you I'm like a window with no glass,
With no way of seeing through.
Without you I'm like a dog with no hairs, to keep it warm.
I miss you like a bird misses its song.
Without you I'm like a school with no children
That chatter and play.
Without you I'm like the Sahara desert with no sand to boil my feet.
I miss you like a washing line misses its pegs,
With no way of hanging clothes.
I miss you like a dictionary misses its definitions,
With no way of telling people what a word means.
Without you I'm like a book without any pages
That people have no way of reading.
I miss you like a printer misses its ink.
I miss you like a child misses its parents
Who love and care for him and
Without you I'm like a human on another planet,
With no way of living.

Daniel Wright (11)
Holland Park Primary School

THE TRAPPER

Working in the coal mine,
He's only six years old,
Starting work at six o'clock,
Down there it's freezing cold,
He opens and shuts a trapdoor,
All day long,
He hears the screaming of the children
And the squeaking of the rats.
The ear-splitting squeals of the ponies
As they are getting whipped,
He opens and shuts a trapdoor,
All day long.

Laura Hart (10)
Holland Park Primary School

HALLOWE'EN

What's that knocking?
What knocking?
That knocking at the door!
What knocking at the door?
Stop it,
Stop what?
Fine I'll answer the door,
Trick or treat!
Ahhhh!
What did you say?
Trick or treat.
What day is it?
Hallowe'en.
What's the time?
Errrrm, 5.30.
What did you say?
Stop it!
Stop what?

Sam Fuller (10)
Holland Park Primary School

MY BOX OF NIGHTMARES

Open the box if you dare!
There's a big hairy spider hidden in there,
With its beady eyes staring at you and
Its body ready to pounce,
There's a snake with a long thin body ready to eat you up,
It will wrap its body around you and make you suffer all night,
There are all the clowns you could imagine with their smiles
That might not be real, running around your bedroom haunting you.
There's all the china dolls watching your every move until
You get so frightened you don't know what to do
And last of all there's a swarm of bees buzzing around your
Room and if you say a word they'll sting you and you'll
Certainly be doomed!

So shut the lid quickly!

Karrin Leach (11)
Holland Park Primary School

HALLOWE'EN

Today is a special day
For it is Hallowe'en
The sky's so dark and black
Yet witches can be seen.
Their hats are pointy,
Their capes are flowing,
They rise and fall,
As the wind blows.
Their cauldrons boil
With newt and bat.
Watching closely,
Their huge, black cat.
Oh I wish, I wish,
I could be flying free,
Oh I wish, I wish,
That witch was me.

Amy Hollis (10)
Holland Park Primary School

THE STARS

As I took a glimpse out of my window,
One cold, windy night,
My eyes saw lovely pictures.
Stars in the night sky look like
Sparkly diamonds glistening on an
Engagement ring.
Gleaming pins sprawled across a wall,
Dots of powdery chalk, splattered on a blackboard,
Holographic sequins scattered over the black velvet cushion,
Beautiful silver buttons shining on a denim jacket.

Chani Antrobus (10)
Holland Park Primary School

THE DOOR

Go and open the door,
There could be something fantastic,
Maybe outside there's a tree with leaves floating down,
Maybe a dog swimming in the sky,
You never know,
Just open the door!

Go and open the door,
You never know what's there,
There could be Spyro the dragon breathing fire,
There could be flowers beginning to grow,
You never know,
Just open the door!

Go and open the door,
There could be something brilliant,
The sun could be whistling and singing,
There could be people chatting and shouting,
You never know,
Just open the door!

Colby Will (11)
Holland Park Primary School

STARS

Stars in the night sky look like masses of xxxx
Showering the page with kisses.
Stars in the night sky look like glitter
Spilt on a black velvet jacket.
Stars in the night look like fireflies
Darting across a river,
Stars in the night sky look like aliens shining torches
On a galactic lake.

Ross Falco (10)
Holland Park Primary School

IAN

It's Christmas time,
The present opening done,
We're off to see my grandad
What fun.

We lock the door,
Now in the car,
We're driving along,
Hadn't gone far.

The skid of wheels,
I jump!
We crash into another car,
I'm lying in a hump.

The flashing of lights,
I do see,
The ambulance man
Is helping me.

Ian can you hear me?
Ian can you speak?
He feels my pulse,
It's very weak.

Rushing to hospital,
It's another place,
It feels like
Outer space.

The pain is horrific,
I try with all my might,
To make it go away,
I sleep for the night.

The pain is gone,
My vision's hazy,
The world's slipping away,
I think I've gone crazy.

At home when I open my eyes,
The nightmare goes away,
Here, my eyes open,
I close my eyes,
I don't see another day.

Adam Gardiner (10)
Holland Park Primary School

THE SOUND COLLECTOR

(Based on 'The Sound Collector' by Roger McGough)

A stranger called this morning,
He didn't leave his name,
Left us only silence,
Life will never be the same.

The crying of the baby,
The purring of the cat,
The ticking of the clock,
The squeaking of the bat.

The ringing of the telephone,
The snoring from my dad,
The sizzling of the sausages,
My brother's going mad.

The popping of the toaster,
The beeping of the bell,
The rustling of the paper,
The gurgling water in the well.

The rustling of the leaves,
The barking of the dog,
The flickering of the light,
Gran tapping on a log.

The moaning of my mum,
The creaking of the stairs,
The drumming of the rain,
The scraping of the chairs.

A stranger called this morning,
He didn't leave his name,
Left us only silence.
Life will never be the same.

Lily Turner (10)
Holland Park Primary School

THE SOUND COLLECTOR
(Based on 'The Sound Collector' by Roger McGough)

A stranger called this morning,
He didn't leave his name,
Left us only silence,
Life will never be the same.

The shaking of the rattle,
The humming of a bee,
The banging of the hammer,
The rustling of the tree.

The barking of the dog,
The purring of the cat,
The crackling of the fire,
The squeaking of a rat.

The tune of the trumpet,
The bang of a ball,
Smashing through a window,
The thump of Dad's fall.

The howling of the wind,
The crashing of a tree falling,
The screaming from my brother's mouth,
The howling of a wolf calling.

The roar of a lion,
The squeaking of a mouse,
The ticking of a clock,
The shouting from my house.

A stranger called this morning,
He didn't leave his name,
Left us only silence,
Life will never be the same.

Eddie Parsons (9)
Holland Park Primary School

WINTER

It's winter at last and snow has fallen,
Snowflakes trickling from the sky,
Cold and breezy, romantic, rotten,
Oh why, oh why.

The pond has frozen over,
Ducks can't swim around,
People are skating and skiing,
Without a single sound.

Children building snowmen,
On the frosty grass,
Teachers getting frustrated,
With the children in the class.

As the weeks pass,
The snow disappears,
Winter has finished,
Hooray! Spring is here!

Claire Hills (9)
Holland Park Primary School

RAPPING RIDING HOOD

Once a little girl called Red Riding Hood
Went to her granny's house deep in the wood.

On the way there she met a fox who
Really liked wearing frilly pink frocks.

She told him she was going to her granny's house,
So the fox crept there as quiet as a mouse.

He gobbled Nan up with not a bone broken.
Now this sly fox was really smoke'n.

When double R H came in the room,
She saw her nanny with a nose like a broom.

Your eyes bulge out, your nose does too
And what's that it your mouth? That's nanny's shoe!

Mean old foxy got out of bed,
Then little Red Riding Hood screamed off her head.

She ran into the woods, like a mad hatter
And everyone was shouting, 'What's the matter?'

Nasty old foxy came out the door;
Saw a bunch of axe men and nothing more.

Matthew Wright (9)
Holland Park Primary School

MY WEEK

On Monday I was born in a brand new world,
I felt like a fresh new leaf.

On Tuesday I took my first step,
A great achievement for me.

On Wednesday I broke my arm,
I was terrified and in pain.

On Thursday I began primary school,
I made friends quickly.

On Friday I found my cat,
It seemed she needed an injection.

On Saturday my grandad died,
I shed an uncountable amount of tears.

On Sunday I wrote these lines,
While looking at the time.

Sam Mahoney (10)
Holland Park Primary School

MY WEEK POEM

On Monday I entered this earth, I
Felt all new while my mum held me.

On Tuesday I learnt to speak
These words, 'Oh no, Mum, Dad
Gone!' My dad and I were
Astonished.

On Wednesday my birthday
Came, I got a brand new bike,
With stabilisers I felt like the
King of the world.

On Thursday I went to hospital
My dad broke his nose,
I felt scared and tearful.

On Friday I paddled in the sea,
A whole new place.

On Saturday I saw my cousins
With my dad, it was fun.

On Sunday, I went to church,
I discovered a whole new world!

Mike Ellmers (10)
Holland Park Primary School

THE PIZZA MAN

The pizza man is short and fat,
He wears a funny paper hat,
All the night and all the day,
He puts the pizzas where they stay,
In his tummy as he thinks,
No wonder that he shrinks and shrinks.

Complaining mothers, grandma too,
Thank God he knows kung fu!
The bills he gives are very scruffy
His dark blue coat is very puffy,
When the pizza man is nowhere,
We all sit down having our share.

Kerry Bray (9)
Holland Park Primary School

SNOW

I awoke especially early on Friday last week
Pulled back the curtains to have a quick peek
Instead of the winter grey, it was bright,
As far as could be seen, everything covered in white!

The excitement rushed through every part of my head,
I awoke the whole family calling, 'Get out of bed!'
'What's all the fuss about?' Mum was crowing,
'Look out the window, it's been snowing!'

I rushed to my dad, but he's just boring
Telling him of the snow, he kept on snoring,
My sisters were excited, just like me
The snow covered everything, even the trees.

I couldn't wait to get out in the street
To feel fresh snow crunching under my feet
To throw a snowball oh so far
Maybe one at Dad, whilst he defrosts the car!

The thought of a snowman standing so tall
That we all could make on returning from school
We'd use coal for his eyes, give him a scarf
We could built it together, we'd all have a laugh.

The schoolday it dragged, every minute felt like an hour
Still thinking of my snowman, as tall as a tower,
The bell finally went, the day finally done,
But the snow had all melted, and now was gone!

Stefanie Klarner (10)
Holland Park Primary School

JESUS CHRIST

J esus was born in Bethlehem,
E ach at the birth of Jesus were the three wise men,
S o the holy bible says,
U tterly enchanted the kings gave him gold, frankincense and myrrh
S tar above the stable is the best.

C hristmas is fun,
H ang up your stocking on Christmas Eve,
R emember that Christmas has a true meaning too,
I t is nice to be with your family on Christmas Eve,
S anta Claus will only come if you're being good,
T o everybody, happy Christmas.

Clare Gravatt (8)
Holland Park Primary School

CHRISTMAS CAROLS

C hristmas pudding at the ready,
H ope all ingredients are there,
R eady cakes are baked,
I t's finally here. Christmas is here,
S anta Claus will come tonight,
T rees are covered with frost,
M erry Christmas everyone,
A gift is coming down the chimney,
S nowing, snowing, outside it's snowing.

C hristmas carols are coming,
A happy tune warms you up,
R eady steady, let's get busy,
O n Christmas songs,
L ights are lit,
S ongs are sung.

Gemma Day (8)
Holland Park Primary School

CHRISTMAS

C   arols singing,
H   appy Christmas,
R   eindeer cheery,
I   cicle freezing,
S   tocking warm,
T   urkey scented,
M   erry Christmas,
A   ngel cheerful,
S   now cold.

Mitchell Freeman (8)
Holland Park Primary School

CHRISTMAS

C hristmas dinner, turkey and gravy,
H olly leaves spiky and prickly,
R ed wine and white wine,
I rregular presents on the floor,
S tuffing is nice and tasty,
T rifle for pudding, yum, yum, yum!
M ischievous Father Christmas opening the door,
A ngel flying in the air,
S nowmen being built in the yard.

Danny Christie (8)
Holland Park Primary School

CHRISTMAS

Christmas time is coming soon,
It is really fun,
We get lots of presents,
There is snow instead of the sun!

We shout out with excitement
And make a lot of noise,
We open our presents
And play with our toys.

We eat our Christmas dinner,
Our family comes round,
I've lost a present,
It has to be found.

Where shall I look?
Under the stairs,
In the cupboard?
Come on and help, no one seems to care!

Look, there it is,
It's in my toy chest,
This is a lovely present,
It is the best.

Amy Wright (9)
Holland Park Primary School

ACROSTIC POEM

S nowballs are the best bit of winter,
N ow all the animals are hibernating,
O utside all the puddles are frozen,
W inter is the best time of the year.
B ig chunks of ice are very dangerous,
A ll the cars are waiting to be defrosted,
L ots of snow has fallen from the sky,
L et's hope it's like this next year.

Ryan Day (8)
Holland Park Primary School

CHRISTMAS

C ards being given to everyone,
H olly spiky and frosty,
R ustling paper coming from Mum's bedroom,
I n the busy road at night,
S anta Claus coming down the chimney,
T urkey cooking in the oven,
M erry Christmas everyone,
A fter dinner, play with brand new toys,
S anta's shadow moving in the dark.

Gaby Baldock (9)
Holland Park Primary School

BOOKS

Tuck into a good book,
Of any sort,
A sticker book,
Or a book on sport.

A book about animals,
Koala bears,
Dolphins and porpoises,
Rabbits and hares.

Get a book from the library,
From any shelf,
A book on history
Or a book on the Celts.

You could get a storybook,
Of any kind,
But make sure,
You like the book you find.

Ellen Gage (9)
Holland Park Primary School

SNOWBALLS

S   now is fun,
N   ow it's winter, we can play,
O   ut in the snow,
W ind is getting cold now,
B   ut it's still fun,
A   snowball and snowmen,
L   aughter,
L   aughter,
S   now is falling.

Tom Childerley (9)
Holland Park Primary School

A BANANA

When I look at a banana I see yellow,
When I touch a banana it is smooth,
I love the taste of a banana, it tastes sweet,
I like the sound of the skin peeling off,
I love to put it in fruit salad.

Gemma Gardiner (8)
Holland Park Primary School

SUMMER DAYS

Summer sunshine
Baking hot
Deep blue sea
Sailing yacht.

Make sandcastles
In the sand
Lie on the beach
Listen to the band.

Have a picnic
Swim in the sea
Banana sandwiches
Now play with me.

Play a game
Have some fun
Skip and chase
Hop and run.

Time for home
Sleepyhead
Fresh hot chocolate
Straight to bed.

Stevie Adams (8)
Holland Park Primary School

AUTUMN DAYS

Noses red
Hands raw
Warm coats
Crunchy floor.

Crackle, crackle
Fireworks leap
Guy burns
Late sleep.

Conkers shiny
Nuts hard
Fruit soft
In a yard.

Hallowe'en
Trick or treat
Witches flying
Pumpkins to eat.

Laura Vile (8)
Holland Park Primary School

Autumn Days

Runny noses
Pink cheeks
Hands raw
Blue feet.

Longer nights
Shorter days
Getting bored
In many ways.

Scary night
Trick or treat
Black cats come
Soup to eat.

Shiny conkers
Chestnuts brown
Eat some nuts
Picked off the ground.

Annabel Shaw (7)
Holland Park Primary School

AUTUMN DAYS

Noses red
Eyes sore
Sneezing loudly
Rain pours.

The weather is dreadful
When the storm strikes
Unhappy fisherman
Waiting for a pike!

The water splashes
On the lake
While the fisherman
Are half awake.

Daniel Curme (8)
Holland Park Primary School

AUTUMN DAYS

Autumn leaves
Gold, orange and red,
Steaming hot cocoa
Then straight to bed.

Hallowe'en is coming
With darker days
Put on your mask
In different ways.

Keep yourself warm
Have a comfy chair
Fragrant shampoo
To wash your hair.

Shaun Buer (7)
Holland Park Primary School

THE MOON

The moon is a shiny football
Without the stitches
The moon is a silver doughnut
Without the hole
The moon is a gleaming eye
Without the pupil
The moon is a yellow conker
Without the skin
The moon is a scoop of vanilla ice cream
Without the taste.

Gabriel Saldin (10)
Holland Park Primary School

SNOW

The crunch of the snow,
The crackle of the children playing on the ice,
The barking of the dog chasing the flakes,
The howling of the wind,
The sparkle of the icicles dangling from the roof,
The smell of roast beef sweets the breezy air,
As more snow falls, the robin calls.

Faye Davis (9)
Holland Park Primary School

MY DOG

My dog barks at the postman,
When he knocks at the door,
He may be little but he has a mighty roar,
His coat is as black as the night,
He would give a burglar a terrible fright.
He loves me I'm sure,
That's why he always gives me his paw,
I walk him every day,
Then it's time for him to play.
I go to bed at 9 o'clock
And on my bed Sooty has his favourite spot.

Laura Gilbert (9)
Holland Park Primary School

POOR SICK BERNARD!

Poor sick Bernard had the flu,
He had to stay at home,
He couldn't go and see his friend,
Cos he would catch flu too.

Poor sick Bernard, still at home,
He hasn't got a clue,
He's lying in his bed right now,
Not knowing what to do!

Poor sick Bernard, I'm worried for you,
I wish you hadn't caught the flu
But my only problem that I have left,
Is that I might have caught it too . . .

Atishoo!

Kirstie Grace Tominey (10)
Holland Park Primary School

THE GOALIE'S SECRET

The goalie's secret is loud and clear,
The aim is to catch the ball,
Like what was practised in the school hall,
As she goes to teach him,
Proud with her pink fluffy slippers running along,
You can imagine the school's song,
'Win, win, win,' cheer the kids,
It works every time,
The goalie's secret,
To save the ball for the school.

Faye Walton (9)
Holland Park Primary School

TEACHERS

Some teachers are good,
Some teachers are bad,
Some teachers are calm,
Some teachers are mad.
Some teachers are wrong,
Some teachers are right,
Some teachers are weak,
Some teachers are full of might,
Some teachers work hard,
Some teachers are lazy,
But in my mind . . .
Most teachers are *crazy!*

Ami-Jane Foweraker (9)
Holland Park Primary School

THE MAGIC BOX
(Based on 'Magic box' by Kit Wright)

I will put in my box . . .
A silky mane of a silver pony.
The sound of waves lashing on the beach.
The silk wool of a red sheep.

I will put in my box . . .
The taste of apple pie.
The taste of freshly baked bread still warm inside.
Fresh, cool water that's been in the fridge.

I will put in my box . . .
The full moon with wispy clouds around.
The sun setting deep, rising out of the sea.
A sandy beach with not a single stone.

I will put in my box . . .
The term breaking up at the summer's start.
The crisp snow falling on the ground.
Warm woolly hats to pull over your ears.

My box is full of secrets and special things to me.,
It's made of shells of magic and the fur of a bumblebee.
In my box I will sleep under a blanket of fire
And wake to find all my dreams have come true.

Hetty Ann Baalham (8)
Mersea Island School

SNOW IS FALLING

S now is falling around and around
N eatly lying on the ground
O utside scene, whiteboard clean
W e like snow falling around and around.

I build big snowballs all day long
S now is like the icing on a big cake.

F alling around and falling around
A big, snowy-white polar bear
L ooking at me
L ooking at me, I'm not your tea
I like snow, but it's going away
N o more snow to be found
G oing away, melting into the ground.

May Leverington (9)
Mersea Island School

THE MAGIC BOX
(Based on 'Magic Box' by Kit Wright)

I will put in my box . . .
A chocolate tree with the leaves smelling of honey.
A flying pig that's flying round the tree.

I will put in my box . . .
The smell of pepperoni pizza just baked
A touch of silky pyjamas and my favourite video.

I will put in my box . . .
Mini people swimming in a glass of Coke
A mini pop star eating popcorn.

I will put in my box . . .
A Monet picture that you can eat
I will also put in my box a chocolate monkey
To go with the chocolate tree with honey leaves
My skeleton that rides a broomstick.

My box is made of all kinds of chocolate
With Smarties around the edge
And caramel stars round the top
I will dance in my box on a stage with lots of lights and smoke
And be the biggest star in the world.

Daisy Sherwood (9)
Mersea Island School

I LIKE SNOW

The fantastic snow is like icing on a cake.
Like tinsel on a Christmas tree.
A winter's white, heavy cloud about to burst
Like a child's snowshaker.
The snow feels like sugar or like sheep's wool.
Like crisp, little snowballs we can make a big snowman
It feels like a puppy's soft, new fur.
Cold little patches of snow
I go and pick it up to play snowball fights with my friends.
I love snow!

Georgina Diprose (7)
Mersea Island School

THE BEACH CINQUAINS

Dawn:
Mud flats:
Salty water
Runs through the squelching mud
While screeching waders search for food
There's none.

Morning:
Wet rocks:
Water surges
Between the slimy rocks
Frothing up silently onto
The shells.

Afternoon:
The shells
The sound of shells
Breaking beneath the sea
Then getting pulled in by the waves
Dragged in.

Evening:
Pebbles
Getting worn down
By the raging ocean
As they slowly drift out to sea
They're gone.

Night:
Silence
As the moon shines
On the deserted beach
Waves drift in and out, in and out
Empty.

Zoe Anthony (11)
Mersea Island School

THE HARD - CINQUAIN

Dawn:
Boats come
Men tie with rope
The men release their ropes
They come back with their load of fish
One ton.

Morning:
People
Come with the trucks
They put the load in crates
The crate goes to the marketplace
They reek!

Afternoon:
People
They go crabbing
To see what they might catch
People might fall in the water
Beware!

Evening:
The day
Is near the end
People let the crabs go
The fishermen tie up their boats
Day ends.

Night:
The nets
They are pulled in
The propellers start up
The fisherman's going again
Swiftly.

Nathan Bond (11) & Ben Baker (10)
Mersea Island School

CHANGES IN LIFE

Harvest is the time of year
When all the crops are gathered
Harvest is the time of year
When brand new seeds are scattered.
The chestnut shells are off the trees
And all the fruits have ripened.
Harvest is the time of year
When we thank the Lord for being our provider.

The countryside is beautiful
A perfect picture of peace;
But man just makes it horrible,
He covers it with litter and grease.
The stretch of waste is immeasurable
It covers a mile at least
The animals are woeful
So make pollution cease.

Thomas Hughes (9)
Mersea Island School

As...

As hot as the scorching fire
As cold as the sparkling ice
As hard as a falling rock from a volcano
As soft as a lovely, cuddly teddy bear
As slow as a tortoise creeping through the fields
As fast as a cheetah running in the long green grass
As wet as the rain drip, drip, dripping off the rooftops
As dry as the yellow grass in the summer
As smooth as silk inside a chestnut shell
As rough as the outside of a conker shell.

Amy-Rose Spurgeon (9)
Mersea Island School

SPREADING THE DISEASE OF WINTER IS FROST

Frost, creating winter in all its tracks.
Coating everything in coldness and frost.
Turning the winds cold and bleak.
Creeping below the darkened, moonlit sky,
With an iced body and frosted rings.
Nothing can be heard but silent footsteps,
Of the only one who roams the lands.
Spreading the disease of winter is frost.

Emily Birch (10)
Mersea Island School

WINTER'S REVENGE

Frost crept through the winter's woodlands,
Under the moonlit sky,
For the rivers turned icy
And the trees stood still,
For it was winter that night,
But nothing could be heard,
Except the whispers of the woods
And the howling of the winds,
For the long night has ended,
But the suffering has just begun.

Charlotte Boyle (10)
Mersea Island School

MR FROST

Frost flew through the dull winter streets.
He walked and everything turned into soft, velvety snow.
Frost darted up in the air and changed the whole world dark.
Frost prowled closer and closer to a child and froze him like prey.
Everything was frozen, except Frost.
He left the world glittery silver.

Sam Ward (9)
Mersea Island School

NIGHT BY NIGHT

Frost stalked peacefully through the snow-covered streets.
The Siberian whispering wind crept into the forest.
The winter's snow reaching out for you, as if a tiger.
Watching the winter nights go by,
Waiting for it to end.

Matthew Wilkin (9)
Mersea Island School

WINTER

Winter prowls the street at night,
While children sleep with cheerful dreams.
The warm elegance of the inn breaks the icy curse.
Animals prepare for the long sleep ahead.
As frost gathers on the icy paths,
Kids are out playing on frozen lakes.

Lewis O'Sullivan (9)
Mersea Island School

WINTER SNOW

Ice walked through the raw winter's night.
Frost stared at the sleety wood,
Cold snow dreamt of the iced forest.
Snow sneaked upon the treetops.
The bleak island was covered in snow.
Snow walked through the winter's night.

Amy Markham (9)
Mersea Island School

GOOD TIMES

Snow covered houses like a gingerbread town,
Winter has crept on the hardened ground.
Children are playing with smiles on their faces,
The snow has given to old people too many new graces.
Snow is a treasure waiting to be found.
Winter crept into the crisp wilderness.
Icicles laid out like hanging jewels.
Frosty mornings from the frosty winter night.
Rivers and grasses all lost under a white blanket.
Good winters have snow and ice.
Good winters have puddings and turkeys.
Good winters have relatives and crackers.
Must I include, good winters have
Presents?

Sarah Taylor (10)
Mersea Island School

WHEN FROST COMES AROUND

Frost creeps through the sleeping town.
Everywhere is frozen stiff, still,
Streams and rivers stop flowing,
When frost comes around.

As night turns into day,
Everywhere glistens and twinkles,
There is no life to be seen,
When frost comes around.

Sophie Moul (10)
Mersea Island School

WINTER

The frosty sound of cold slipping
Through the streets leaving a white sheet.
The dead silence sends jeopardy through the street.
The suppleness of snow is as bitter as the North Pole,
The magical white sheet turns to ice,
Everything it meets.

Jack McKinlay (10)
Mersea Island School

WINTER'S NIGHT

Frost slipped through the icy forest,
Cold flew above the frozen town,
Snow walked on the arctic peaks,
Ice danced through the winter landscape,
Winter crept through the icicle woodland.

William Manning (9)
Mersea Island School

WINTER COMES

Frost crept over the snowy houses.
Snow silently walked over the frosty towns,
Cold slid over the frosty people.
Ice turned all the lakes as solid as rock.
Icicles hung from the frozen gutters.
Frozen house windows as solid as ice.
People sitting by the warm fire.

Thomas Calcutt (10)
Mersea Island School

WINTER

The frost crept into the snow-covered inn.
Winter covered the gloomy street.
Frost coldness hid from the warm.
Cold covered the house all white.
The winter froze the big sea.
The powerful wind froze the stream.
The wind blew into homes and made everyone cold.
Snow made the bridge all white.

Ben Cirne (10)
Mersea Island School

WINTER WONDERLAND

Winter walked through autumn
Making everything a frost.
Rivers are like glass.
Nuns are skating round and round on the pond.
Snowmen are melting,
The ice is unsafe.

Caitlin Devonish (9)
Mersea Island School

WINTER'S DAY

Frost crept through the snowy street with a soft sound.
Cold touched the white covered forest.
Snow walked into the frosty garden.
Ice ran through the black of the night.
Icicles skipped through the icy road.
Wind flew through the frosty river.
Winter crept through the cold wood.

Billy Riley (9)
Mersea Island School

SNOW IS FALLING

Snow is falling, coming down fast.
Children rush to see what the noise is about.
Icicles drop from the walls,
I feel a chill going down me,
The paths are slippery all along.
This day is finished, I'm moving on.

Lucy Cook (9)
Mersea Island School

THE WINTER POEM

Icicles frozen upon the rooftops
Icicles spiked along the trees.
Cold snow crept along the treetops,
Frost upon the icy rivers.
Winter raced with cold wind.
Winter crept with frost and cold
Ice slivered upon the icy floor,
Snow is cold like frost.

Rebecca Cole (9)
Mersea Island School

WINTER IS COMING

Long icicles fly over treetops.
Cold is swimming by homes and towns.
Frost is coming to look for ponds to ice.
Snow has tracks and footprints.
Ice looks like tinsel everywhere.

Natasha Lawrence (9)
Mersea Island School

AL SNOW

Ice flew through the streets making cold.
It covered the paths and roads
Making it slippery and hard to drive through,
Because of Al Snow.
Al Snow - half person, half snowman.
Snow falls when he's happy.
Black ice comes to mean war.
Al Snow clutches and flips,
But it only lasts a matter of time.

Glen Sales (9)
Mersea Island School

MR SNOW

Mr Snow slithered through the cold winter's night
And changed everything he saw to snow that was soft as silk.
He flew through the dark cold winter's street turning water into ice.
Mr Snow landed and made streets slippery.
He flew back up and saw the glistening world.

Danny Lavender (9)
Mersea Island School

THE WINTER NIGHT

Snow fell from the shadowy sky,
The sign of winter.
Ice covered the pond,
Icicles came to hunt.
Trees have frozen and winds shivered,
All the streets quivered.
Leaves on the trees freeze,
Crushed by howling walls.

Megan Gibbons (10)
Mersea Island School

APPROACHING

Smoky breath, bitter ink and tar
Dark gloomy eyes, blind as a dungeon
Purple, twisted body covered with a hundred marble-sized warts
Creeping out of the dark shadows
Searching for its next, weak victim
Pounces, grabs and attacks.

Nicholas Menzies (8)
St Mary's CE Primary School, Kelvedon

WINTER RECIPE

Take eight screaming, numb hands
Mix in flowing wind
Beat in shiny icicles
Sprinkle decorated Christmas tree
Put some chips of a frosty, brown bench
Stir in seven cold, white snowmen
Leave in the cold
For three long months
And you have made winter!

Anna Goodchild (7)
St Mary's CE Primary School, Kelvedon

A VANISHING MONSTER

Cold, stinky breath like a rotten, stale chicken
Enormous green eyes
Brown scaly skin covered with huge spots
Freezing cold hands
Long, sharp nails
Roaring like a tiger
Grabs a little barking fox
Vanishes into a gloomy, huge, foggy forest.

Robert Beardmore (8)
St Mary's CE Primary School, Kelvedon

THE MONSTER WITH FIERY EYES!

Breath like rotten vegetables, stinky and stale,
Fiery eyes, a crackling flame in each pupil,
Scabby, scaly skin, silver in the moonlight,
Tiny feet, a giant, hooked claw, leaning out of each bent toe,
A low, whispering voice, a drum in each word,
A tall, twisted body, just visible in the mist,
Slowly crawls out of his slimy, dark cave,
Waddles to the nearest village,
Kills five unsuspecting children
And disappears back to his gloomy cave.

Catherine Borgartz (7)
St Mary's CE Primary School, Kelvedon

THE MONSTER FROM HELL!

Stale fish breath, rotten eggs and manure,
Slime-green eyes shining, sharp like broken glass,
Purple, pimply skin covered with throbbing warts,
Red ferocious claws to rip its prey to pieces,
Roars like an angry lion running to the kill,
Gigantic muscular body to ram and stun its prey,
Climbs up from a fiery hell and abducts a poor, defenceless child
And disappears in a sheet of smoke.

Oliver Stead (8)
St Mary's CE Primary School, Kelvedon

The Spotty Monster From The Stone Castle

Cold, stale breath,
Which smells like burnt toast.
Blood-red fiery eyes,
Staring evilly, waiting to grab its prey.
Skin covered in huge, red spots,
Thick, sticky pus flowing out.
He flies out of his stone castle,
Snatches a helpless lamb
And soars into the wintry air.

Alice Shield (7)
St Mary's CE Primary School, Kelvedon

A WINTER RECIPE

Take a Christmas tree, add presents underneath
Pour in a field of cold, falling snow
Use a warm, crackling fire to warm you up
Put a red-checked jolly snowman in with cold, wet snow
Shake in a big snowball fight
With glistening frost and slippery ice
Stir a silent dawn with a quiet season.

Lewis Williams (8)
St Mary's CE Primary School, Kelvedon

WINTER RECIPE

Take a collection of warm, woolly clothes
Add a big snowball fight
Pour in hot radiators
Chop some salty paths
Mix in some indoor games
Whisk in lots of coats on the coat pegs
Decorate with a Christmas celebration
Beat in a non-stop snowfall
And an extra cold, shivering season
Leave in the glistening frost
For three long months
And that's my recipe for winter.

Alice Warby (7)
St Mary's CE Primary School, Kelvedon

A Recipe For Winter

Take a field of falling, gentle snow,
Pour in a chest of fluffy, cosy clothes,
Chop some icy trees to put on the hissing fire
Mix in a scrumptious Christmas dinner
With a fat, overflowing stocking
Stir in glittering, freezing ice
Leave in the deep snow
For three long months
And you have made winter!

Amelia Fletcher (8)
St Mary's CE Primary School, Kelvedon

CELTS V ROMANS

People creeping up on our enemies,
I can hear soldiers crashing into others,
All I can see is bodies dead on the floor,
It looks like Hell.
I feel frustrated, angry and most of all,
I am a cold-blooded killer.
I can feel men groaning and moaning and sad.
I can hear screaming and shouting,
We are running,
We are running,
To our friends.

Amy Jo Miles (9)
St Peter's CE Primary School, Coggeshall

SNOW

Snow is falling,
Birds are not calling,
Fields are white.
Snow has laid,
Children have made
Snowballs all for a fight.
It's not warm,
It's just like dawn,
Winter's day is light.

Snow's stopped falling,
Birds are calling,
Fields are clear.
Snow has thawed,
Children are bored;
Their snowballs quickly disappear.
Countryside has warmed,
Morning has dawned,
Spring's day is near.

Verity Michie (8)
St Peter's CE Primary School, Coggeshall

OH WHAT A HORRIBLE WORLD!

Oh the smell is disgusting!
Oh what a horrible pong!
Why do people do this to the world,
To the Earth,
To the air we breathe?

Oh the sight is atrocious!
Oh what a terrible place!
Why do people treat the Earth like this?
Like a dumping ground,
A place no one cares about?

Sometimes I wonder,
What the Earth used to look like,
Before we came along,
Before we destroyed it
Before we made it a disaster.

When the skies were the bluest blue
And the sea was the greenest green,
The Earth must have been beautiful,
More beautiful than the prettiest lady,
Better than ever before!

Oh why,
Oh why do people treat the Earth like this?

Katie Watts (10)
St Peter's CE Primary School, Coggeshall

SNOW ON THE MOUNTAINS

Snow on the mountains
Whiter than unicorns
Just wait until it rains

Sparkling in the sun
Whiter than white icing
It's only just begun

Glittering snow falls
Whiter than this paper
Gently muffling my calls

Huge twinkling snowdrift
Whiter than sparkling eyes
It's big; it will not shift

A glistening dome
Whiter than winter frost
Covering the shrew's home

Sheets of skidding ice
Whiter than a bright light
Hiding the sleeping mice

Fluttering showers
Whiter than the fluffy clouds
Wet and cold: its powers

It just never stops
Whiter than even white
Snow on the mountain tops

Catherine Jones (10)
St Peter's CE Primary School, Coggeshall

CASTLE MOOR

Upon one stormy evening at Castle Moor,
A charge of soldiers armed with bows,
Also some swords, the war was going to Moor.
As soon as I arrived there were bodies.
Bodies were covered in lots of blood and gore.
The war had ended and neither side had won,
It started there and ended there, upon Castle Moor.

Tommy Styles (10)
St Peter's CE Primary School, Coggeshall

SNOW HAIKU

Snow is glitter dust
Snow glistens in the sunshine
In the morning light.

Ice is see-through glass
Ice is slippery-slidy
Ice is wet and cold.

I like the snow days
I like sliding on glass-ice
It looks beautiful.

Blue skies, powdery snow
Glittery hills on the ground
Perfect, no footprints.

Sunny day, cold ice
Shining clear, cold shimmering
A mirror of ice.

The snow melts away
Ice turns into crystal drops,
Summer is coming!

Eleanor Unsworth (11)
St Peter's CE Primary School, Coggeshall

SNOW, PLEASE DON'T GO AWAY!

I was at home waiting for snow,
That's the white and fluffy stuff,
That we throw around,
We make snowmen with it
And have snowball fights,
Snow, please don't go away!

I know it's pretty cold,
But I like rolling it around;
And when you're not looking,
Ouch!
I throw a snowball,
Snow, please don't go away!

The snow has finally come,
I'm going outside to play,
Put on my gloves and boots,
Come and join me, brother,
Let's have a snowball fight,
Snow, please don't go away!

It was snowing all day,
It was snowing all night,
Now it is five inches thick!
I made a glittery angel,
Chris made a naughty devil.
Snow, please don't go away!

The snow is melting,
The ground is turning brown.
The white is getting muddy.
Please don't go away!
Snow, don't go away!
Oh no! It's gone!

Caroline Howe (9)
St Peter's CE Primary School, Coggeshall

EATING IN CLASS

One day I went to school,
I was so hungry that I ate my pencil
And I had a bite of my shoe.
Mmm! I thought
That was nice!
Then at break time the teacher had left his shiny red apple,
So when he went out, I took it.
Uh oh!
But I was still hungry.
The teacher said, 'Where's my apple?'
'It's probably under your chair,' I said.
He looked,
'No it's not.'
I said, 'I ate it,'
And that's that.

Kristi Taylor (8)
St Peter's CE Primary School, Coggeshall

THE STORM

The trees are falling
Their roots in the air,
I close the curtains
Not daring to stare.

The lightning striking
All around,
The grass sizzling
On the ground.

When the sun comes out to stay,
That's when I go out to play!

Alasdair Plumb (9)
St Peter's CE Primary School, Coggeshall

MY SNOWMAN

I am building a snowman, here I go,
Gathering up lots of snow.
When I've finished I'll stand back proud
And look at my snowman stuck to the ground.
It is white and fluffy, bright and cold,
If I touch it, it will be cold,
Well, so I've been told.
Then my mum came out to see what I had done
And I said, 'Look it's a snowman, Mum!'

Daisy Miller (8)
St Peter's CE Primary School, Coggeshall

SUMMER HOLIDAYS

As the bell at school is rung,
The holidays have begun.
There are four of us in our gang,
Me, Kate, Liz and Little Ann.

So we went to the park,
Before it got dark.
Then my brother Jimmy-Lee,
Butted in (he's a pain, you see!)

So he decided to take us swimming,
Me, Kate, Ann and Liz.
Mummy couldn't take us,
She was looking after Granny Wiz.

We whizzed down flumes,
Me, Liz, Kate and Ann.
My brother went on the big one,
The Daredevil Dan.

He accidentally broke his nose,
My brother Jimmy-Lee.
It was on the 3rd bend,
(He went down headfirst, you see!)

So now we're playing in my yard,
(Without Jimmy-Lee.)
He's in bed, all tucked up,
With his nose in plaster, you see!

Robyn Strachan (9)
St Peter's CE Primary School, Coggeshall

FUMES AND DUST

Abandoned cars
by the hour
on the road and on the grass
like dead trees, rotten and mouldy,
it makes you wonder.

Factories old and falling down
next to the bright green field
like a pile of rubble,
it makes you wonder.

Litter everywhere you look
next to the old oak tree
like a blanket of snow,
it makes you wonder.

I see the abandoned cars
I see the old falling down factories
I see the litter
Day by day,
are you wondering too?

Rhys Sanderson & Mason Melling (11)
St Peter's CE Primary School, Coggeshall

THE ROBOTS' XMAS DINNER

When the robots came to dinner
They came on Xmas day,
They wouldn't eat the *turkey*
They threw it all away,
They ate up all the knives and forks
And then they asked for more.
We've never had a Xmas dinner like that before.

When the robots came to dinner
They came on Xmas day,
They wouldn't eat the *vegetables*
They threw them all away,
They ate up all the knives and forks
And they asked for more.
We've never had a Xmas dinner like that before.

When the robots came to dinner
They came on Xmas day,
They wouldn't eat the *stuffing*
They threw it all away,
They ate up all the knives and forks
And then they asked for more.
We've never had a Xmas dinner like that before.

When to robots came to dinner
They came on Xmas day,
They wouldn't eat the *Xmas pudding*
They ate up all the knives and forks,
Then they asked for more.
We've never had a Xmas dinner like that before.

Jessica Mitchell (10)
St Peter's CE Primary School, Coggeshall

EARTH

The air is blowing as I tie my lace,
The sea is gushing as I start my race.
The sun is shining so warm on my skin,
It's a shame our ozone layer's wearing so thin.
The fishes swim in a world that's wet,
Then along came the fishermen with their net.
The baby animals aren't allowed to grow,
Is this the world we want to know?
Is it a problem or is it not?
Do we have time to stop the rot?

Luke Cobbold (8)
St Peter's CE Primary School, Coggeshall